Prayer for the op

A premium trac

James A. Thome

Alpha Editions

This edition published in 2024

ISBN 9789361476570

Design and Setting By

Alpha Editions

www.alphaedis.com

Email - info@alphaedis.com

Contents

SLAVERY UNCHRISTIAN.

There is a deep and growing conviction in the minds of the mass of mankind, that slavery violates the great laws of our nature; that it is contrary to the dictates of humanity; that it is essentially unjust, oppressive, and cruel; that it invades the rights of liberty with which the Author of our being has endowed all human beings; and that in all the forms in which it has ever existed, it has been impossible to guard it from what its friends and advocates would call *abuses* of the system. It is a violation of the first sentiments expressed in our Declaration of Independence, and on which our fathers founded the vindication of their own conduct in an appeal to arms. It is at war with all that a man claims for himself, and for his own children; and it is opposed to all the struggles of mankind, in all ages, for freedom. The claims of humanity plead against it. The struggles for freedom every where in our world condemn it. The instinctive feeling in every man's own bosom, in regard to himself, is a condemnation of it. The noblest deeds of valor and of patriotism in our own land, and in all lands where men have struggled for freedom, are a condemnation of the system. All that is noble in man is opposed to it; all that is base, oppressive, and cruel, pleads for it.

The spirit of the New Testament is against slavery, and the principles of the New Testament, if fairly applied, would abolish it. In the New Testament no man is commanded to purchase and own a slave; no man is commended as adding any thing to the evidences of his Christian character, or as performing the appropriate duty of a Christian, for owning one. Nowhere in the New Testament is the institution referred to as a good one, or as a desirable one. It is commonly—indeed, it is almost universally— conceded that the proper application of the principles of the New Testament would abolish slavery every where, or that in the state of things which will exist when the Gospel shall be fairly applied to all the relations of life, slavery will not be found among those relations.

Let slavery be removed from the church, and let the voice of the church, with one accord, be lifted up in favor of freedom; let the church be wholly detached from the institution, and let there be adopted by all its ministers and members an interpretation of the Bible—as I believe there may be, and ought to be—that shall be in accordance with the deep-seated principles of our nature in favor of freedom, and with our own aspirations for liberty, and with the sentiments of the world in its onward progress in regard to human rights, and not only would a very material objection against the

Bible be taken away,—and one which would be fatal if it were well founded,—but the establishment of a very strong argument in favor of the Bible, as a revelation from God, would be the direct result of such a position....

There is not vital energy enough; there is not power of numbers and influence enough out of the church to sustain slavery. Let every religious denomination in the land detach itself from all connection with slavery, without saying a word against others; let the time come when, in all the mighty denominations of Christians, it can be announced that the evil has ceased with them for ever; and let the voice from each denomination be lifted up in kind, but firm and solemn testimony against the system—with no mealy words; with no attempt at apology; with no wish to blink it; with no effort to throw the sacred shield of religion over so great an evil—and the work is done. There is no public sentiment in this land—there could be none created—that would resist the power of such testimony. There is no power *out* of the church that could sustain slavery an hour, if it were not sustained *in* it. Not a blow need be struck. Not an unkind word need be uttered. No man's motive need be impugned, no man's proper rights invaded. All that is needful is, for each Christian man, and for every Christian church, to stand up in the sacred majesty of such a solemn testimony, to free themselves from all connection with the evil, and utter a calm and deliberate voice to the world, AND THE WORK WILL BE DONE.

REV. ALBERT BARNES.

CALL FOR A PRIZE TRACT.

The subscriber is authorized to say, that a friend, not wishing his name should be publicly known, offers $100 to the person who will write the best tract on the duty and importance of praying for the abolition of slavery and oppression, especially in our own country, particularly adapted to interest new converts before their minds become embarrassed with political and party strife.

The tract is to be entitled, "Prayer for the Oppressed." The offerer nominates and requests the gentlemen named below to act as committee of award, to wit: Rev. Elnathan Davis, Fitchburg, Mass.; Rev. George Trask, Fitchburg, Mass.; John W. Sullivan, Boston, Mass.; Charles B. Wilder, Esq., Boston. Mass.; Rev. E. H. Nevin, Chelsea, Mass.

The tract should not exceed 24 pages of common size when printed, and should be sent to the committee of award in season to be examined, and the prize one transmitted to the publication committee of the A. T. S., Boston, by the 1st of June next.

NOAH EMERSON,
For the offerer of the Prize.

HOLLIS, N. H., January 21, 1859

Last winter, a Christian gentleman, by advertisement in the New York Independent, offered a premium of $100 for the best tract which might be submitted on *"Prayer for the Oppressed."* The undersigned were nominated and requested to act as a committee of award in this case, and have received and examined a large number of manuscripts, many of which were of marked ability and power; but finding no *one* of these so fully to answer the call of the offerer of the prize as to allow them to award the whole of it to *that*, they have awarded the same in equal divisions, to the authors of the *two best* manuscripts, viz.: Rev. GEORGE W. BASSETT, Washington, D. C., and Rev. JAMES A. THOME, of Cleveland, Ohio. And they have strong confidence that these tracts will soon come before the public, and that God will mightily bless them as an instrumentality in inciting the Church universal to benevolent action and believing prayer, for the overthrow of slavery and oppression.

ELNATHAN DAVIS,

EDWIN H. NEVIN,

GEORGE TRASK,

JOHN W. SULLIVAN,

C. B. WILDER.

BOSTON, August, 1859.

PRAYER FOR THE OPPRESSED.

Who are the oppressed? Those who suffer wrong from the more powerful. They are to be found in all conditions of society, in the bosom even of the family and the church. All relationships which involve authority are liable to be abused to the infliction of injustice and outrage.

Who are THE OPPRESSED, distinctively? *The enslaved.* These differ from all other victims of abused power in this essential point, that, by the law, they are regarded not as *men,* but *things,* the property of men. Denied humanity, they are denied all human rights, and excluded from all human relations. They have under the slave code as administered, no legal protection; the show of it which the letter of the law, in some instances, affords, being designed rather to guard their value as property than their interests as men.[1] Outcasts in society, they are outlaws in the State.

Overlooking this vital distinction, many persons hold that slavery is one of the legitimate social relations, and therefore not in itself a proper subject of censure; while its grievous evils, the result of the abuse of rightful power, may justly be deplored. But others, with a closer discrimination, discern that the "chattel principle" which characterizes slavery is inherently wrong, and that it is the chief promoter of the spirit of oppression. It is believed that if slavery were abolished, oppression would thereby be materially diminished throughout society. Holding this view, the people of God are earnestly combating the slave system. The moral power of the church, wielding the pulpit and the press, has been increasingly arrayed against this stupendous wrong. A more perfect combination of the forces of Christendom for the overthrow of oppression is devoutly to be wished. But this will not avail without the power of God. That power must be invoked,—must be secured. The servants of the Most High, who would have him honored and his cause promoted by the extinction of slavery, must cry unto him day and night,—must give him no rest, till he come and deliver the oppressed. Fully persuaded of this, we wish to urge—

The duty and importance of praying for the abolition of slavery and oppression.

1. The fitness and effectiveness of prayer as a weapon against slavery claims attention.

It would be powerless in such an extreme case if it were in itself a feeble instrumentality. But all things are possible to prayer. What is the scriptural idea of prayer? This; it is the offering to God of desires which his own

Spirit has kindled in the heart, with importunities which the same Spirit prompts and sustains; it is also made with humble reliance on the merits of Jesus Christ, and the prevalence of his intercessions. Prayer, then, is not the work of man alone; he is but a co-worker with God in this, as in every other gracious endeavor,—with the Holy Spirit dwelling in his heart and moving him to pray, and with Jesus the Mediator who presents his supplications at the Father's throne. This is the view of prayer which our Lord discloses in John 15:7, 16, Paul in Rom. 8:26, 27, and James, also, 5:16; "The effectual fervent prayer of the righteous man availeth much." It availeth much, not because it is offered by a righteous man, but because it is effectually and fervently inwrought by the Holy Ghost, who dwelleth only with the righteous. The power of Elijah's prayer is referred to in the connection, to illustrate and confirm the statement that all real prayer is mighty. Elijah had no more power than other good men may have; he had the infirmities common to the servants of God, but the strength of Jehovah was with him; that strength was in his prayer; and so it may be,—must be,—in all prayer.

The power of prayer, then, is God's own power, exerted by the Spirit and the Son through the supplications of the righteous, and therefore it availeth much. Nothing can withstand it, because nothing can withstand God. The elements of nature yield to its control; the institutions of men, founded in sin, fall before its cry.

If slavery were beyond the power of prayer, it would be not because of its strength, but because it is right in the sight of God. And if it be right, the Spirit will not move the righteous to pray for its abolition. If God be for it, who can be against it?

Let us then inquire whether this be a proper subject of prayer?—whether a system of bondage which degrades man into a beast of burden and of traffic is pleasing or hateful to God? That it exists, and has endured for ages, is no evidence that it enjoys his favor. Sin exists, and has prevailed from the beginning. Romanism flourishes, and has had the ascendency in Christendom for fifteen centuries. Idolatry reigns, and the kingdom of Satan looks down from its ancient seats scornfully on the kingdom of Christ. Among the most dreadful exhibitions of God's wrath and vengeance have been those in which he has, with a high hand and an outstretched arm, delivered the oppressed, and destroyed their oppressors.

Slavery is the foe of Christianity, the enemy of souls, and it must be hateful to the God of love, who would have all men come to Christ. It is opposed to the gospel and to every evangelical work, to the tract, the Bible, the missionary enterprise. It disregards the spiritual interests of enslaved saints, and of souls perishing in their sins under its yoke. It is a ruling power in this Christian country, to the scandal of religion. It rises above other forms of sin, as the chief perverter of the right ways of the Lord. It hinders the spread of vital godliness through this land, walling about the dominions of its chattels and excluding the preacher of the cross. The Christianity it tolerates within its borders is not that which declares the whole counsel of God; which cries aloud and spares not, and shows the people their sins. The religion of America, fraught with salvation for the nations of the Old World, has been shorn of much of its power by the encroachments of Southern slavery. Can any Christian doubt that a system so hostile to the gospel is abhorred of God? And now, at this moment, the issue is forced upon us, whether slavery shall exclude the gospel, or be excluded by it. In this crisis our only help is in God. We must be persuaded that he will defend his gospel, and humble the slave power.

Note this, that slavery is not one of those organic vices of society which are to be left to the reformatory influence of Christianity operating silently upon them, but is rather an *opposing force* to be directly and resolutely met, in the name of the Lord. In the advance of civilization, ignorance is gradually dissipated, but savage violence is to be encountered at once and subdued. In the school, the family, the nation, the church, certain evils admit only of indirect treatment, but others call for decisive, positive measures. Slavery in a Christian republic preëminently demands direct action, aimed at its speedy extermination. It may long resist such action, but no other is pertinent to its nature. When, after the Revival of 1830-33, the attention of the people of God, especially of the young converts, was turned to this subject, they proclaimed the truth—Chattel Slavery is a sin, and immediate emancipation is the duty of the slaveholder. With this battle cry *the institution* was attacked by a host of witnessing warriors clad in the armor of God. That onset had undoubtedly a divine origin, and the principle that animated it was a true one, that slavery was to be swept away in righteousness. And had the entire weight of Christian power sustained the assault, and had the united energies of the saints in prayer been secured, the quarter of a century that has passed would probably have witnessed the downfall of the "peculiar institution." But many leading minds in the churches thought it best to let slavery alone, and to leave it to the slow but sure influences of Christianity, by which it would be eventually extinguished. Twenty-five years have demonstrated that this grievous system of oppression is not undermined by the gospel, nor weakened by revivals. It has made most rapid strides, and is now far more defiant of religious powers than ever before. Shall not the teachings of the past suffice to prove that in dealing with slavery nothing is to be gained by *indirection*? Is it not time now, after the late gracious revival, to renew and reassert the declaration—Slavery is sinful, and must be abolished? Let this voice be raised; let it be echoed by all the churches; and let the saints carry to the throne of grace, and urge with faith and boldness this plea,—"Great God! abolish slavery." This prayer will be acceptable, and will prevail, if God, as we are sure he does, hates this stupendous sin.

2. The duty and importance of praying for the abolition of slavery appears from this—that if prayer does not prevail against slavery, slavery will disarm prayer of its prevailing power, and reduce it to an empty form.

It is an accredited maxim that "praying will make us leave off sinning, and sinning will make us leave off praying." The reason is obvious, and the application is plain. If indulging sin in the heart is inconsistent with cherishing there the spirit of prayer, the allowing of any prevalent sin in society, on the ground that it is beyond the power of prayer, is equally inconsistent. For this is to admit that its removal is impossible with God. The alternative is forced upon us,—either slavery must be overcome by prayer, or prayer be foiled by slavery. These two powers now stand opposed to each other.

This is providential, and fraught with vital consequences; as when Goliah and David met. Slavery is to test the strength of prayer, the faith of Christians. Which shall prevail? Is the Slave Power too strong for prayer, or have the saints such faith and argument touching this thing, that they may ask what they will, and it shall be done? It is a first principle of evangelical faith, that, "all things are possible to them that believe." If this principle is yielded, the foundations of prayer are removed. If *any* thing is impossible, nothing is possible; faith that fears is dead, and prayer that quails is powerless. If the servants of the Lord flee before the formidable front of chattelism, instead of compassing it with mighty prayer, and dragging it before the Lord to be slain, they will betray a fearfulness which must preclude all acceptable prayer. The great God loveth strong intercessors, strong and bold, who "wrestle not against flesh and blood,"—weak foes; but "against principalities, against powers, against the rulers of the darkness of this world, against spiritual wickedness in high places,"—"praying always with all prayer in the Spirit." The only aristocracy in Christ's kingdom is composed of the princes who have power with God and with man, and all who will believe may wear the title of this order, "Israel." But they must believe *only*, "lifting up holy hands without wrath or doubting." They must believe only, not mixing fear with faith, nor trying with trusting; that trying which first scans the magnitude of a sin, estimates its power, and counts the cost of assailing it. The faith that prevails in prayer has its sphere above the calculations of difficulty and danger, where sense fails, and strength staggers. It is just as easy for believing prayer to take hold of great things as of small. The little English girl, languishing in her mortal sickness, when she was told that Bonaparte was preparing to invade her country, could grasp that national peril in her hourly prayer; and who will say that the threatened invasion which might have changed the fate of Great Britain was not averted in answer to that dying child's intercessions?

Side by side in the Lord's Prayer stand the petitions, "Thy kingdom come; Thy will be done on earth as it is done in heaven;" and, "Give us this day our daily bread." No topics could be more dissimilar in magnitude, yet God hath joined them together, and the believer passes easily from the greater to the less. But let the petitioner put these asunder, and pray for bread alone, as deeming the other too great a favor to ask for, and his prayer will not prevail. God is honored by that fearless, resolute faith which says, "Who art thou, O great mountain? Before the Zerubbabel of prayer thou shalt become a plain!" This great mountain of slavery is the providential provocative in our day of the prayer of faith which removes mountains. The aspects of it which most dishearten man do most arouse against it the spirit of prayer. "Is any thing too hard for God?" Is slavery too great for the Almighty? We must either pray against this national sin, or limit the Holy One to minor evils. We dare not do the latter, we should fear to pray at all. To every intercessor coming to the mercy seat, the gracious King says, "What is thy request?" And if, despite the pressure of the times, no mention is made of the crying wrong of oppression, he is grieved, and turns away. It is as if queen Esther, going into the presence of the king, with the fate of her doomed people claiming her entreaties, had feared to ask so great a favor as that their doom might be averted, and had only craved for herself a new chariot, or a larger retinue of servants.

In this view of the subject, it is painful to reflect that the theme of supplication which for twice ten years God has been urging upon his people has been so strenuously excluded from the prayer meeting, the monthly concert, and the sanctuary. Who can say how provoking this has been to the Hearer of prayer, and how often it may have rendered the petitions of his saints an abomination unto him? Had not the Holy Spirit, with more than human forbearance, borne with the manners of the people, and laid the unwelcome burden on their hearts, and inwrought fervent desires, impelling many to pray earnestly for the oppressed, there might by this time have been little more than the form of prayer in the American Zion. Yes, prayer for the oppressed has done much to preserve the vitality of prayer in the churches! This has been its happy reflex influence, although it has had to struggle against much gainsaying of misguided brethren. When it shall have prevailed against slavery, and wrought out the deliverance of them that are in bonds, then will be seen, as now is not, the irresistible power of prayer. We rejoice in the assurance that prayer will overcome slavery. We have no fear of the alternative. We are glad to have this decisive test applied. Let it be seen in this crisis what the prayer of faith can endure, and what it can do. It has other trials to overcome, other triumphs to win.

3. The importance of prayer for the abolition of slavery in this country, is shown from the inefficacy of other means to effect it.

Every other mode of opposition has been vigorously employed. The first minds of Christendom have written and spoken against this monster iniquity. Its champions have been forced to acknowledge, "The literature of the world is against us." But oppression laughs at literature,—it defies the rostrum and the press. The moral influence of the nation has borne against it with a pressure seemingly irresistible; State and national anti-slavery societies with the motto, "agitate, agitate, agitate;" mass meetings hurling the thunders of popular indignation; Christian conventions uttering the reprobations of religion; notes of warning from dying patriots; appeals to justice and humanity from honored philanthropists; remonstrances from the purest divines; the entreating voice of Christian women;—all these moral forces have borne against slavery. But it mocks at moral suasion. Political measures have been tried,—tried in good faith and with the utmost energy. But the Slave Power, versed in the intrigues of politics, has gained victory after victory, and grown stronger by this species of opposition. Providential events have signally fought against slavery. The successive acts of European powers have swept chattel slavery from their colonies. Cuba and Brazil, with our own country, alone retain it. Repeated emancipations by individual slaveholders at the South have kept alive the anti-slavery feeling. The violent measures which the slave power has employed to fortify and extend its dominions have exasperated and alarmed the people of the North. For a quarter of a century this movement of the people, of the churches, of political machinery, sustained by favoring providences, has been in progress; yet slavery in America is mightier to-day than it was at the beginning of the movement.

Do not these facts show the duty and importance of prayer? We are prone to try everything else before we resort to wrestling prayer. We *have* tried everything else. We have prayed, indeed; but chiefly to crave God's blessing on our other measures. *This will not suffice.* In such a desperate case, prayer must take hold on the arm of the Lord, and move it to strike the decisive blow. We must be convinced that only the Lord can break every yoke, and bid the oppressed go free; and we must realize that he will be inquired of to do this thing. Not discarding other means, we must give the preëminence to this. We must pray and faint not. Each believer must alone intercede for the oppressed. Bands of implorers must join in heart as touching this thing, and with full agreement and faith beseech God to abolish slavery. Intent on putting to the proof this last remedy, let the Christians of America establish concerts throughout the land, for closet and for social prayer. Let prayer be accompanied with occasional fasting, in token of humiliation, for the sin of oppression. This demon can be cast out, but not without prayer and fasting. Christ is able to rebuke the evil spirit, and to bid it come out of the nation. His disciples have been trying to exorcise it, and have failed. Let them take the case to him, and see if he will not work a deliverance. When he takes it in hand, and speaks the word, there may indeed be a deadly struggle, and the fell spirit, ere he departs, may rend the nation and fling it on the verge of dissolution; but he who is strong to deliver is also mighty to save. We need not fear the issue. Do not some really dread abolition more than slavery? The remedy is worse than the disease, they think. But should Christians distrust the cure which their Redeemer would effect? Here, perhaps, faith is most tried,—to commit this work of abolishing slavery to the Lord, and to have him cut short the work in righteousness. It may be we have been secretly determined to keep off the dreaded event which we are sure must come at last. They who have been foremost as abolitionists and immediate emancipationists may do well to examine themselves on this very point; peradventure they are not, after all, prepared to see slavery abolished at once! Where stand the people of God generally touching this issue? Are they ready to trust the case in his hands? Are they prepared to have every yoke broken, and to see the oppressed set free? Can they be agreed to pray for this unconditionally, dictating no terms?

4. That prayer for this object should be made without longer delay, is proved by the extreme dangers of the continuance of slavery, and of the strife it occasions.

Do we apprehend the evils of sudden abolition? We had better consider the perils of prolonging chattel slavery in this land of liberty. "Oppression maketh the wise man mad." Only the brutish man will long endure brutal treatment himself, or tolerate its infliction upon another. If despotism breeds disaffections, slavery begets insurrections, as light enters the house of bondage. And the light is advancing—fearfully. Appalling dangers are just ahead. The mixed race is rapidly increasing. The hottest blood of the South flows in the veins of slaves, who are often scarcely distinguishable in complexion from their oppressors. Abolition deferred may come too late. Provocations, slight compared with those of slavery, drove our fathers to rebellion. The worst passions are inflamed by the atrocities of the chattel system. The revolting scenes of the inter-State slave trade, the abominations of slave breeding, the barbarities of the cotton field and rice swamps, the ferocities of the slave hunt with blood-hounds in the South, and with more savage men in the free States, the imprisonments and lynchings of Northern men found in the slave States and suspected of holding abolition sentiments, the many collisions between slavery and freedom, which have in some instances proceeded to bloodshed and death, have caused much irritation and deep indignation throughout the country. Freemen are exasperated; good people are aroused; the moral sense of the nation is shocked and tried to the utmost. The sentiments of patriotism, devotion to the Union, and respect for federal law, are lowered in the public mind. Faith in free institutions, and hope of their perpetuity are seriously shaken. Sectional animosities are rife. The republic is no longer a unit, for the hearts of the people are sundered. Issues the most radical divide us: freedom and slavery! There is determination on either side, and strong feeling. There can be no reconciliation and no respite in this fraternal strife. Nothing can end it but the removal of slavery. Only this can avert the evils that now threaten the republic. Emancipation or ruin is the alternative which the tide of events is forcing on us. It is now a time of trial, a crisis. The elements are fraught with trouble. Peacemakers are abroad, but agitators are stronger than they. This is no time to cry peace. Men behold the oppressions that are done under the sun, done under "the stars and stripes," and they are stirred. There is no leisure for speculation and conjecture. Let no time be wasted in idle fears, or in useless efforts at pacification. The conflict must continue; God wills it! Let his people commit the cause to him. Let them betake themselves to prayer.

And what shall be the burden of their supplications? Shall they pray for peace, for a calming of the waters, for a putting out of the fires of freedom which burn against oppression? No, no! Let them pray *for the abolition of slavery*. Let them not mock God by calling upon him to stay the work which his providences have so manifestly been pushing forward. Where are the intercessors who, in God's light, see light on this subject, who are prepared to enter into the divine plans, and who will please the Lord by asking him boldly, in faith, to put an end to slavery? Where are the wise and discerning men, in whom is the Spirit of the Lord, who clearly see that this is the only salvation to all the interests of American liberty? Let them speak out, and summon the saints to repair without delay to the throne of grace, in this time of need.

By the several considerations foregoing we would urge the duty and importance of praying for the *abolition of slavery in America*. We would lay this solemn duty on the hearts of Christians; we would earnestly entreat them to stir themselves to take hold on God for this great blessing to the nation and the world. We would humbly say,—Brethren, quench not the Spirit, which may now be moving you to pray, and may be waiting to work in your hearts the fervent and effectual prayer which, poured forth by the help of his intercessions and unutterable groanings, will avail much. Make full proof, beloved, of the power of prayer. A better test there could not be. Let it be seen that prayer can overcome slavery. Make it manifest that what the literature, the moral suasion, and the political action of one generation has not done, the prayers of God's people can do. Important interests await this result—the nation rescued from ruin, Christianity saved from apostasy. Emancipation gained by prayer will avert emancipation wrought by violence.

Slavery done away in righteousness, oppression in its other forms will be meliorated and will gradually disappear. The apprentice, the clerk, the sailor, the soldier, the pupil, the child, the laborer, the hired girl, the wife, will be more secure from the abuses of power, when the spirit of oppression, driven from its stronghold, is shorn of its strength. The abolition of slavery in this country will go far to drive the spirit of oppression out of Christendom, and to liberate the nations of Europe.

Such results, rationally to be anticipated, should certainly impel Christians to pray. The purity, the peace, and the prosperity of Zion are so implicated, that to pray for the abolition of slavery is to pray for these. The power of revivals, the success of home and foreign missions, the operations of tract and Bible societies would be increased immeasurably by the overthrow of slavery, and by the augmented strength this victory would practically give to prayer. The available energies of the American Zion would be multiplied many fold. The Bible would be vindicated, Christianity would have the trophies of the triumph, and God would gain great glory.

Oh! then, who among the saints will restrain prayer?—Who will come not up to the help of the Lord against the mighty? Who will incur the bitter curse of Meroz? Rather, who will not bear some part in this faith-struggle at the throne of grace? Who will not share in the rewards which God will bestow on his people, when he comes to avenge them speedily by the overthrow of slavery? What praying circle, what pulpit, what concert or closet, will be found wanting in this crisis?

Prayer for the abolition of slavery involves *prayer for the oppressed*. Ungodly men may oppose slavery, and yet have little sympathy for the enslaved; but the Christian can not bear the sin of slavery to the throne of God without bearing thither the wrongs and woes of the oppressed. Moralists may condemn chattelism in the abstract; but they who are moved to pray by the Holy Ghost will "remember them that are in bonds as bound with them."

"*Who are the oppressed?*" we asked at the outset, and answered, The enslaved. Again we ask, Who are the oppressed? Who are these victims of slavery? Who are they that we should pray for them? We answer:

They are *men*. They belong to the human family. They are of one blood with ourselves. They have the same rights with us, the same interests, the same desires, the same wants, the same love of liberty, the same sense of right and wrong, the same deathless spirits. The negro in his chains appealingly interrogates us,—"Am I not a man and a brother?" What can the Christian do but own the relationship? Is he indeed a man—a brother? Then does not to him the golden rule apply—"Do unto others as ye would they should do unto you?" *Can* we exclude them from our prayers?

They are *innocent* men. By no hideous crime against humanity have they forfeited their place in the brotherhood. For no violation of law have they been consigned to bondage. Against them, rather, has all law been violated, and every dictate of humanity outraged. Guilty only of a colored skin, and of inevitable ignorance, they have been doomed to abject servitude. From birth they have been made property. In their infancy they knew no mother, but merely a nurse; in their childhood they had no home; in their maturity they have no companions, and no children, but merely offspring, like the brutes. Yet, they are innocent men. Sinners indeed they are before a holy God, as are all mankind; but they are innocent of *crime*. They are oppressed without cause. What should hinder the prayers of the righteous in their behalf?

Many of them are *the children of God*, by regeneration. These are our brethren in the Lord, one with us in Christian bonds, "fellow citizens with the saints, and of the household of God." They cry day and night unto God, and their cry enters into his ear. Our blessed Saviour would have us pray for and sympathize with these his little ones, as we love him. He is very pitiful towards them, and very jealous toward those who slight them. Realize that they are their Lord's, that they are not their own, that they can not be the property of their owners, that they are bought with a price. Regard the enslaved saints as the Lord's freemen; that their Master hath need of them; that they are forbidden to call any man master, on earth, for one is their Master, even Christ. *Can* it be the will of Jesus that his own redeemed saints should be held and treated as beasts? Will he not be grieved if his followers who are free, pray not for the freedom of these their brethren in bonds? When Peter was put in prison in Jerusalem, "prayer was made without ceasing of the church unto God for him," and it wrought his deliverance. Let prayer be now made without ceasing by the church, for the liberation of all enslaved saints, and enlargement shall surely come. The living God waits to be importuned by the church for its own members. He waits to hear the cry of distress from Zion, suffering with her suffering children.

The unconverted slaves are hopeful subjects of renewing grace compared with the same number of any class of men. No persons on earth are more susceptible to gospel influences than the negroes. What the missionary has labored almost in vain to effect among the Indians, among the Jews, among the Catholic immigrants in this country, would, we are confident, be done with large success among the slaves of the South, if they were emancipated. Strike off the shackles, and this Ethiopia would stretch forth her hands unto God.

The oppressed are *a great multitude. Three millions of souls* are crushed and brutalized by slavery. Three millions of souls are robbed of every human right, and subjected to every abuse and cruelty that the caprice, lust, or cupidity of the slaveholder may dictate. The master is wholly irresponsible. The slave plantation is a petty, absolute despotism. From thousands of fields the blood of the oppressed crieth to God for vengeance. Millions of groaning, sighing wretches are appealing to Heaven for mercy. With these groans of the enslaved will mingle the prayers of the righteous in their behalf; and no doubt the Lord will hear.

The oppressed are to be regarded as having wants while in their bondage which God only can supply; but it must be borne in mind that the their great want is *freedom*. Let this be sought instantly, importunately. Beware of praying for them as slaves, as if their condition were unchangeable; this were a grievous insult to God and to humanity. Pray for the oppressed—that they may go free. Pray for the oppressors—that they may break every yoke. Pray for the missionary and the colporter—that they "may open their mouths boldly, to make known the mystery of the gospel; that therein they may speak boldly, as they ought to speak." We may be sure that God will not suffer the oppressors long to stand between his salvation and the souls of the oppressed. We may plant our feet on this firm assurance when we pray,—"The Lord will open a highway for his word." If he sends his messengers to the south to preach salvation, he will stand by them and will give their word success, though their blood flow to seal their ministry.

Let it not be, O brethren, that our prayer for the oppressed shall be less fervent because they are not of our own color; lest it should appear that we have "the faith of our Lord Jesus Christ, the Lord of glory, with respect of persons." Were this so, how could the Spirit of prayer dwell at all in our hearts? It were a crying wrong if *prejudice* should restrain prayer for the enslaved. He who has no pity for the bleeding bondman because he is an African, is not like the good Samaritan, is not like Christ, who died for all men, is not like God, with whom is no respect of persons.

And let not our prayers be hindered by fears of what may come after emancipation. The faith that is adequate to prayer is also able to commit the results of God's action to his management. It is to be feared that some have become discouraged by the growth and ascendency of the slave power, and have no faith that prayer for the oppressed will avail. Their trust is in political action, or in the judgments of a just God, and the vengeance of the oppressed. Be not, beloved, drawn into this attitude of unbelief and "fearful looking for of judgment and fiery indignation." *"Be not afraid; ONLY BELIEVE."*

What shall be the bearing of the late revival upon slavery? It is a signal fact that each great awakening in this country, including that of 1797, has been marked by the arousing of God's people to the sin of oppression.

We have already spoken of the influence of the outpouring of God's Spirit in 1830-33, as giving rise to the great modern movement in opposition to slavery. Simultaneously with this, a strong dislike of it on moral grounds was seizing many minds at the South. Various demonstrations of this were made by religious bodies; and in some of the slave States emancipation was seriously meditated and openly proposed. The writer of this tract, a native of the South and a member of a slaveholding family, religiously trained to regard slavery as scriptural, and expecting to be, after the manner of his father, a church member and a slaveholder for life, was hopefully numbered among the subjects of the revival of 1830. He consecrated himself to the work of the ministry. The spirit of prayer was given him, with yearnings to be holy and to be useful. His eyes were then opened to the moral condition of the slaves. He saw those of his own household, though his father was a ruling elder in the Presbyterian church, living without God, without religious instruction, without moral restraint; he saw the young slaves, the fruit of promiscuous concubinage, the playmates of his childhood, and scarcely of a darker hue, (though happily claiming no blood relationship, as those of some Southern families do,) growing up in ignorance and vice. Deeply moved, he cried unto the Lord that he would save their souls. He daily prayed for those miserable creatures; he nightly bathed his pillow with tears of pity and distress. But he found no relief; he saw no ray of hope. He dreamed not then that slavery itself was wrong, and that its abolition was the only remedy for the ills of the oppressed. He knew not that many others were moved as he was, and that it was the Lord who was thus stirring the first impulses of a mighty movement for the redemption of the enslaved. Just then, a tract, or pamphlet, sent by some unknown hand from the East, was taken from the post-office. It was on the safety of immediate emancipation. The very subject riveted attention by its novelty and boldness. The tract was read in secret, and read again, and soberly pondered. Light broke in; new thoughts, new feelings, new hopes were inspired. In less than one year, (1833,) the writer was a member of Lane Theological Seminary, and an avowed convert to the new doctrine.

These were some of the fruits of the revival a quarter of a century ago. They have lasted till now. Opposition to chattel oppression in this country is in great measure due to that gracious work, and to the spirit of prayer which has sustained and sanctified it. Surely we can not doubt that God is in this movement. Another mighty revival has been enjoyed by our American Zion—the most powerful, perhaps, of the series. It has been specially characterized by the spirit of prayer, which has been poured out in large measure, and has wrought astonishing results.

It is now a momentous question: To what ends shall this renovated instrumentality of prayer, in the hands of a revived church, and of a multitude of young converts, who owe their hopes to it, be applied? Against what forms of sin and evil shall this weapon be wielded? What embodiment of wrong most invites this species of attack, by its opposition to everything vital in godliness? Is it not American slavery? We assuredly gather that it is God's will there should be a special and combined effort in prayer, to pull down this stronghold of iniquity. We have confidence that the Holy Ghost, who has given the saints a fresh baptism of prayer, will incline them to unite their supplications against this abomination.

Christian reader! Will you not bear this burden to your closet? Will you not make the bondman's wrongs your own? Christian parents! Will you not mingle with your thanksgivings that your children were born free, importunate supplications that the curse of slavery may be removed from every family in the land? Young converts! Ye who, in answer to prayer, have been liberated from the bonds of sin, will you not plead with God to deliver the oppressed, and to abolish slavery? Ministers of Christ! Will you not call upon the Lord, "praying with all prayer and supplication in the spirit," and leading the sacramental host to the throne of grace? Are there Christian households, and Christian sanctuaries in this land, where the oppressed have not been habitually remembered in prayer? Are there disciples who have not sympathized with the sighing bondmen? Are there "women professing godliness" who have been deaf to the wail of slave mothers sundered from their babes? Let these things be no longer, lest the cry of the down-trodden millions call down swift retributions. May the spirit of grace and of supplications be poured out upon Zion, until liberty shall be proclaimed throughout all this land, unto all the inhabitants thereof. So God grant for his Son's sake!

FOOTNOTES:

[1] The following is a decision of the Supreme Court of Kentucky. Kentucky Reports, p. 644. JUDGE SHANNON—"Slaves, although they are human beings, are, by our laws, placed on the same footing with living property of the brute creation. However deeply it may be regretted, or whether it be politic or impolitic, a slave by our code is not treated as a person, but (*negotium,*) a thing, as he stood in the civil code of the Roman Empire."

FROM A SERMON BY REV. E. N. KIRK, D. D.

In addition to the reasons urging to prayer for the extinction of slavery growing out of the character of the system, and the condition of the oppressed, there are other reasons derived from its influence upon the slave owners.

Of these there are three classes: the unwilling master—the willing, but kind master—and the oppressor.

1. I know of no condition so full of trials as that of the slave-owner who abhors the relation, but does not see that he can properly terminate it. That there are many such can not be doubted. But what a life must a godly man lead who has come to comprehend its enormous wickedness! What must be his apprehensions of the wrath of God upon his people, his country! If a man of skeptical views, like Jefferson, could tremble for his country in remembering that heaven is just, what must he feel who fully believes that God is ruler among the nations, and that he hates oppression! How painful must be his unavailing sympathy for the poor oppressed beings whom he sees around him! How must his heart be burdened as he observes the demoralizing influences of slavery on both races; how often must his love of country be pained with that just contempt which slaveholding in America excites in every civilized nation under heaven; how painful must it be to see no relief in any quarter, but, on the contrary, everything indicating that the system is to be incorporated into the whole civil and social system of the nation! And to crown all, while many intelligent persons at the South would gladly abandon slavery, no man has the courage to utter his sentiments.

This class of slave-owners demands our deepest and most compassionate sympathy.

2. There is another class who have been taught from infancy by their parents, teachers, and pastors, that slavery is a divine institution; they see no wrong in it, and consider all the evils as incidental, and not as legitimate consequences of the system. They are the most powerful upholders of it, because they believe it to be right, and are conscious of no other than kind sentiments towards their slaves. To such men and their sentiments the oppressor triumphantly appeals as an evidence that slaveholding is not injurious to character, nor repulsive to the feelings of good men.

3. Then there is the oppressor—the man in whom slaveholding is a sin *per se*. He holds his brother as property. He denies to man, for selfish ends,

the rights and prerogatives of manhood. He denies that the possession of life, liberty and happiness, or the unobstructed pursuit of them, is the right of every man unconvicted of crime.—But not to rest in general statements, let us place side by side some facts, and some passages of the word of God.

The facts are that slavery robs a man of his humanity. He is made a thing, a chattel, merchandise. The African has no right on earth but to do the will, and promote the comfort of the Caucasian. He can not choose his residence, his employer, his work. He can not receive wages or the fruits of his industry. He can not defend his wife against insult. He can not protect his children from violence. He can not live with his family if it does not suit the interests of another man. He can not educate his children. He can not choose an employment for them. He can not hope for anything but slavery. He can not worship God when he pleases. He can not testify in a court of justice.—Now what does God think of all this? "I hate oppression," is his reply. "Remove not the landmarks of the widow," he says, "their cry will come before him; their Redeemer is mighty." "Go to, now, ye rich men, weep and howl; the hire of the laborers who have reaped down your fields which is of you kept back by fraud, crieth; and the cries of them which have reaped are entered into the ears of the Lord of Sabaoth." Not a day, not an hour probably passes in which some oppressed petitioner is not filing his petition in the chancery of heaven against the slave-owners of our land.

We have probably had more indignation than sympathy for these men. And yet they are to be pitied. Probably none of us have been as deeply indignant at the sins of oppressors as Moses was at the idolatry of his people at the very base of Sinai. And yet when the Lord threatened to cut off Israel and raise up the promised nation from him, he prayed thus for them: "Forgive their sin;—and if not, blot me, I pray thee, out of thy book which thou hast written!"

We can not then have exhausted the duty of prayer for the overthrow of oppression till our sympathies and intercessions have embraced the slave-owners as well as the slaves.

And there are peculiar encouragements for seeking the abolition of slavery by prayer.

1. God's special readiness to hear prayer when his people are in straits. Notice the sketches of personal and national history in the Bible. How many of them are recorded in order to show how ready God is to deliver his people when in their perplexities they cry unto him. Jacob, Moses, David, Hezekiah, Mordecai, Nehemiah, the church in Jerusalem when Peter was in prison. "Now these things were for our ensamples."

2. The time of terminating an infliction has come when it has produced an humble and hearty return to God.

3. The mode of deliverance thus secured will be the best. An end might be put to slavery by a civil war; but the remedy would be unspeakably worse than the disease. But suppose the church of God to take up this matter with an humble, united heart; and before the world and God become, like Moses, an intercessor, and ready to employ other means subsequently and subordinately, we can not doubt that slavery would come to an end; and then observe with what blessed results:

What glory to God! He will be acknowledged as holy, as gracious, as powerful, as a hearer of prayer.

What benefits to the slave! Liberty, elevation, knowledge, all social and civil blessings.

What relief to the master!—from crime, from the consciousness of wrong-doing, from fear, from a bondage of dependence, unthriftiness, and numberless vexations.

What blessings to the country! Asperities all softened. North, South, East and West united in one brotherhood; the nation honored in the approbation of the world; Freedom a grand reality for all.

What advantage to the cause of Christ! Christians henceforth one; wounds healed; the way of usefulness unobstructed; the church hastening with united strength, and with the blessing of God, to the spiritual conquest of the world!

IS HE NOT MAN?

Is he not *Man*, though knowledge never shed
Her quickening beams on his neglected head?
Is he not *Man*, though sweet religion's voice
Ne'er made the mourner in his God rejoice?
Is he not *Man*, by sin and suffering tried?
Is he not *Man* for whom the Saviour died?
Belie the Negro's powers! in headlong will,
Christian, *thy* brother thou shalt prove him still.
Belie his virtues! since his wrongs began,
His follies and his crimes have stampt him Man.
Montgomery's West Indies.

WRONG OF SLAVERY.

My ear is pained,

My soul is sick, with every day's report

Of wrong and outrage, with which earth is filled.

There is no flesh in man's obdurate heart;

It does not feel for man; the natural bond

Of brotherhood is severed as the flax

That falls asunder at the touch of fire.

He finds his fellow guilty of a skin

Not colored like his own; and having power

To enforce the wrong, for such a worthy cause,

Dooms and devotes him as a lawful prey.

I would not have a slave to till my ground,

To carry me, to fan me while I sleep,

And tremble when I wake, for all the wealth

That sinews bought and sold, have ever earned.

No; dear as freedom is, and in my heart's

Just estimation prized above all price,

I had much rather be myself the slave,

And wear the bonds, than fasten them on him.

Cowper's Task.

No. 42.

Milton Keynes UK
Ingram Content Group UK Ltd.
UKHW050244220624
444555UK00005BA/510